This delightful gothick doocot at Megginch, Tayside, dates from 1809 and marks the centre of a court of offices. The galleon weathervane is reputed to be a model of the ship on which Captain Drummond of Megginch sailed to India in 1783. The diamond window is a dummy; the pigeons gaining access through 'ports' below the pointed arches.

SCOTTISH DOOCOTS

Tim Buxbaum

Shire Publications Ltd

CONTENTS

Introduction 3
The beehive pigeonhouse................ 5
The lectern doocot 7
Architectural designs 11
Disenchantment with pigeons 17
Farmyards and courts of office 19
Composite and miscellaneous
    structures 24
The twentieth century 26
Further reading 29
Gazetteer of doocots..................... 30

Set in 9 point Times roman and printed in Great Britain by C. I. Thomas & Sons (Haverfordwest) Ltd, Press Buildings, Merlins Bridge, Haverfordwest, Dyfed.

British Library Cataloguing in Publication Data available.

ACKNOWLEDGEMENTS
    The author wishes to express his gratitude to the Society for the Protection of Ancient Buildings and the Royal Incorporation of Architects in Scotland for their encouragement of research into Scottish doocots, and he is grateful for the co-operation of a number of local authorities and landowners in Scotland for their help in locating and visiting doocots.
    All the photographs are by the author, as are the sketches, some of which were first published in an article about 'Scottish Doocots' in *Out of Town* magazine, June 1985.

Dolphinton doocot, Lothian, is of the three stage beehive type. The stages are separated by rat courses. The remains of a glover can be seen on the roof.

The square plan doocot with an unusual timber glover at Ballindalloch, Grampian.

INTRODUCTION

The Romans kept pigeons in a *columbarium* or *peristeron*, which could hold as many as five thousand birds, and men were paid to chew bread which could subsequently be used as a superior kind of pigeon feed. The pigeons were 'crammed' and quite often their legs were broken to fatten them more quickly for the table. Varro, in *Rerum Rusticarum,* wrote of five requirements for keeping pigeons. These were shelter, ventilation, ease of access, protection from vermin and the provision of nesting facilities, and they have remained virtually unchanged ever since.

Pigeonhouses were widely built all over Britain, but the pattern of distribution in Scotland, where they are known as doocots, was dependent on the availability of richer arable lands which could support settlement, so there were always more examples in Fife and East Lothian than, for example, Argyll.

In the feudal society of the early fifteenth century, the pigeonhouse was considered the legal right in Scotland of all abbeys, monasteries, castles and baro-

nies. The earliest castle doocots were probably very ordinary timber structures, but early ecclesiastical structures were impressive enough; in the fifteenth century the second floor of the tower of Inchcolm Abbey was converted to a pigeonhouse, and even the old central tower of St Columba's Cathedral, Iona, offered accommodation for the birds. Church towers were also utilised, the 'doos' being the property of the minister, sometimes to the distress of the congregation, which complained of the mess.

Early legislation encouraged the construction of doocots and offered protection to the owners. In 1424 it was decreed that 'destroyers of pigeonhouses' were to be punished as severely as 'stealers of green wood by night' or 'peelers of bark to the destruction of the trees', and the penalty was a fine to be paid to the king. Further laws followed, and in 1503 the parents of children who broke into pigeonhouses risked the fine of two-thirds of a pound, whilst the child would be given up to a judge to be 'leschit, scurgit and doung according to his fault'.

In the same year King James IV of Scotland directed all lords and lairds to help the community by building deer parks, stanks (for fish), cunningaries (for rabbits) and pigeonhouses, but many people resented the pigeons which ate the crops they toiled to raise, and further laws had to be passed in an attempt to protect the birds. By 1567 shooting at the laird's pigeons was punishable by forty days in prison, and a second offence might mean the loss of one's right hand. Under King James VI penalties became even harsher: eight days in the stocks and a £10 fine for a first offence rose to a £40 fine for a third offence. If he did not pay the offender was likely to be 'hung to death'. Even sentences as harsh as these did little to deter the hungry poor.

For the laird there were many good reasons for having a pigeonhouse. Eggs and young pigeons, or peesers, could easily be gathered from nesting boxes set back into the walls of the structure and the adult birds could be caught in nets, to provide fresh meat at times of the year when much else would be dried, smoked, salted down or preserved in pickle. In those days much livestock was slaughtered in November, since there was no winter grass for feed. At any time of year, when other food supplies were

The early beehive doocot at West Meikle Pinkerton, Lothian. (Upper) The walls are of rubble with a few dressed stones around the entry door and pigeon ports. (Lower) Stone nesting boxes line the thick walls. The doorway is low for maximum security and to deter birds from flying out when the door was opened.

4

threatened by enemies, the pigeonhouse was a very useful resource.

Pigeons would be at their plumpest and best in September when the food supply was at its peak, and they could be stuffed with garlic and stewed, or simmered in a 'twice-baked pie' with a double crust of suet and pastry. Squab pie was for many years a national dish in Scotland. A recipe from the mid seventeenth century suggests that the birds should be baked in a pot with claret for ten hours, after which they could be sealed with butter and kept for up to three months, and the *Cook's Oracle,* published in 1818, mentions other dishes where an entrée of pigeons might be arranged 'in the form of a spider...a frog...' or even 'in the form of the moon'.

There were uses other than as food. The copious droppings on the floor of the pigeonhouse could be collected to yield fertiliser, and Batty Langley recommended 'pigeon dung cast thin upon cold lands in the Spring is very helpful, especially for corn and meadow lands'. It was discovered that pigeon dung, being rich in potassium nitrate, could be mixed with black earth and sulphur to produce a form of gunpowder. Pigeon dung could also be used in dyeing cloth and as part of the leather tanning process.

The laird, therefore, had a considerable asset in his pigeonhouse, and one that did not require a great deal of maintenance. When he got bored it would even provide him with some useful shooting practice. News of at least one Scottish battle was delivered by means of a homing pigeon, and in later years fanciers would do much to breed specially decorative birds with ruffs.

THE BEEHIVE PIGEONHOUSE

Early references suggest there was a bronze age pigeonhouse at Skara Brae in Orkney and *Pococke's Tours* refers to a pigeonhouse formed from a Pictish dwelling on Hoy, also in Orkney. A doocot at Ballencrief in Lothian was recorded in the thirteenth century, and at 'Robert the Bruce's Library' at Hawthornden pockets that may well be nesting boxes are cut into the walls of a cavern.

There are a number of naturally formed 'doo caves' on the rocky coasts of Scotland, for example near East Wemyss in Fife, and some of these were almost certainly 'improved' in medieval times. The first purpose-built structures that we commonly think of as doocots, however, are the sixteenth-century 'beehive' doocots, named after old-fashioned straw bee-skeps. Scotland's oldest surviving doocot may be the one built into the walls of Crossraguel Abbey. Some people claim that the oldest *dated* doocot is one at Mertoun House, but the datestone of 1576 may have been reused from an earlier structure.

The typical beehive pigeonhouse is of circular plan, some 3 metres (10 feet) internal diameter, built up in massive rubble construction of three or four 'stages' to a shallow domed roof, often finished with an ornamental billeted cornice and crowned by an open cupola or *glover* for pigeon access. Human access, at ground level, would be through a small but heavy door, checked into dressed quoins, leading directly into a single chamber surrounded by stone nesting boxes, one for each pair of breeding birds, with up to a thousand boxes in a large structure. Vermin were deterred from climbing the walls by projecting stone 'rat courses', which had some ornamental value.

In the centre of the chamber of some beehive doocots and most of the later varieties a revolving ladder provided access to the nesting boxes so that eggs and birds could be easily gathered. The ladder is called a *potence* and is made up of an *arbre* and a *gallows pole.*

Most beehive doocots are somewhat clumsy looking, squat and rather heavy, but the examples at Aberdour, Mertoun House and Nunraw Abbey have a certain elegance.

ABOVE LEFT: *A beehive doocot built into the walls of Crossraguel Abbey, Strathclyde.*

ABOVE RIGHT: *The squat, rotund and massive typical beehive doocot at Luffness, Lothian.*

BELOW LEFT: *The fine doocot at Aberdour, Fife. Unusually, five steps lead down into the chamber.*

BELOW RIGHT: *The beehive doocot at Phantassie, Lothian, with a built up roof for protection from the weather.*

6

The doocot at Spott House, Lothian is a typical lectern type of generous proportions with a nice steeply pitched roof.

THE LECTERN DOOCOT

The beehive design was superseded in the sixteenth and seventeenth centuries by doocots of square and rectangular plan, which had much greater flexibility. Some doocots built around 1600 (for example, Tealing, New Spynie) were of squarish plan with a pitched roof rising to a central ridge, the entire construction being of stone. Much more efficient, and more common, was the timber and masonry 'lectern' design. The main characteristic of the lectern type is the monopitched roof, usually south-facing, with crow-stepped gables on which the pigeons could perch and preen. The lectern design had two principal advantages over the beehive type. Firstly, the interior could be divided into two or occasionally four separate chambers (for example, Leitcheston), each lined full height with nesting boxes of stone, brick or timber. Each chamber could be independent of the others, reducing disturbance to the birds from constant visits and offering increased security. Some additional security might be provided by the use of double doors (for example, Waterybutts)

or by a moat. The second advantage of the lectern design was that its more sophisticated construction made it more suitable for decoration. Marriage stones, heraldic panels and armorial designs (for example, Pinkie, Dumfries House) were integrated with rat courses that became moulded and organised into string courses which could also be used as alighting ledges for birds. Ball finials, sundials and carved heads were worked into designs which included cusped and crenellated gables, and flight holes (or pigeon ports), could be formed into dormers and fitted with shutters or hooks for nets. Later pigeonhouses even included arrangements whereby a rope at the entry door could be pulled to shut the pigeon ports to prevent the birds escaping at collecting times. Such refinements, and especially the suggestion of ostentation and flamboyance, underlined the increasing importance of the doocot to the laird.

Doocots became so popular that by 1617 the right of owning or maintaining a pigeonhouse was limited by statute to lairds whose lands produced each year

Tantallon Castle, Lothian, right by the sea, is the setting for one of the oldest lectern doocots. It has two chambers and is of crude and massive construction.

'ten chalders of victual', or about 10 tons. Only one pigeonhouse could be built for such a measure, but there was no limit on size or location, provided that it was sited no more than 2 miles (3 km) away from the owner's land. Hardly any doocots seem to have been demolished under the 1617 legislation, though there is some evidence that flight holes and nesting boxes were on occasion sealed up.

Stocking a pigeonhouse seems to have been something of an art. Kidnapping of neighbours' birds may have occurred from time to time, but generally methods

LEFT: *At Drumquhassle, Central region, the doocot is a pleasant lectern type, dated 1711, in a particularly fine setting.*

BELOW: *Johnstounburn House, Lothian. Detail of a life sized lead pigeon poised on the roof of the doocot. It must have been designed as a decorative decoy.*

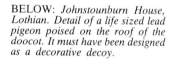

RIGHT: *The doocot at Glamis Castle, Tayside, is unusual in that the back wall has been built up as a feature to give additional shelter from the winds.*

LEFT: *At Pinkie House, Lothian, is this early example of a two-chambered lectern doocot. There are decorative panels above the doors, including a 'marriage stone' referring to Alexander Seton and Margaret Hay, wed in 1607.*

RIGHT: *Westquarter doocot, Central region, with its fancy decoration, is now in the middle of a housing estate.*

LEFT: *One of the most sophisticated designs of lectern doocot is at John-stounburn House, Lothian. At first floor level inside there are over 2000 nesting boxes. The noise must have been tremendous.*

9

were more honest, or at least fairly subtle. A spiced dog, roasted with cumin, and a 'salt cat' were mentioned as suitable lures to induce pigeons to take up a new home. More pleasant is the suggestion that anointment with myrrh, or old wine and cumin mixed with grain, might sweeten the breath of a few resident pigeons and persuade others to move in. By 1735 a 'salt cat' probably just meant a mixture of saltpetre and cumin with sand and lime. It was considered unsportsmanlike to hang mirrors round a doocot and count on a pigeon's natural vanity to encourage it to leave a former nest. Nevertheless there are life-sized pigeons of lead, wings outstretched, poised as if to launch themselves into the air from the skews of the doocot at Johnstounburn.

A good deal of mystique and superstition grew up about doocots and pigeons. The 1725 edition of *The Sportsman's Dictionary* suggested the use of tin plates fixed to the outward walls of a pigeonhouse to deter climbing vermin. The theory was that rats would lose their grip and fall to the ground, to be impaled by iron spikes.

The lectern design still survives in Scotland as the commonest form of pigeonhouse but most have little practical use today and many are now ruinous. Developments in the eighteenth century fundamentally changed the form of the doocot once again, and it is ironic that the lectern style was revived in the 1970s, in characteristic if not in detail, as 'modern vernacular' style housing for humans.

LEFT: *Cutaway drawing showing a potence or revolving ladder which would be positioned at the centre of the doocot as an aid to gathering eggs and young birds.*

RIGHT: *Addistoun, Lothian. Cutaway drawing of the unusual two chambered lectern doocot with only one entry door. Access to the further chamber was probably under a false floor about 3 feet (0.9 m) above ground level.*

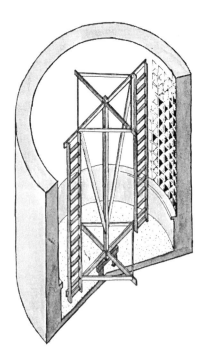 

Daldowie, Strathclyde. (Left) The great circular doocot is built of red sandstone finished with an unusual slated roof. At present it enhances a sewage works. (Right) Inside hundreds of stone nesting boxes are lit by a hole in the roof. The central revolving pole of the potence is clearly visible but the ladders have perished. The base of the pole turns on a block of stone.

ARCHITECTURAL DESIGNS

There was a saying that the meagre inheritance of a Scottish laird was 'a puckle land, a hantle o' pride, a doocot and a law plea'. From 1707 onwards, unless he was a Jacobite, his prospects might have increased considerably. 1707 was the date of the Act of Union between Scotland and England and it marked an increasing desire for unity and stability between the two kingdoms. Although political unrest and even bloodshed continued, there was increasing optimism among landowners in Scotland who had sympathy with England. Established landowners and those who benefited from the acquisition of confiscated Jacobite estates were anxious to develop and improve their lands, and during the eighteenth century there were vast changes, including the evolution of the country seat.

A growing atmosphere of optimistic pragmatism manifested itself in Scottish arts and humanities and was particularly noticeable in agricultural improvements and landscaping. Major planting schemes were initiated which would in time produce great avenues of trees striding over the landscape to frame views which might focus on a mountain, a lake, a little temple or even a doocot. Pleasure grounds were enclosed by walls, and if a village happened to be in the way it was simply razed and rebuilt elsewhere.

In 1727 Sir John Clerk of Penicuik wrote *The Country Seat,* a long poem praising the change in contemporary taste from formalism to naturalism; this was four years before Pope's *Epistle to Lord Burlington* about 'the genius of the place' and consistent with Sir John's recognised position as an arbiter of taste in Scotland.

11

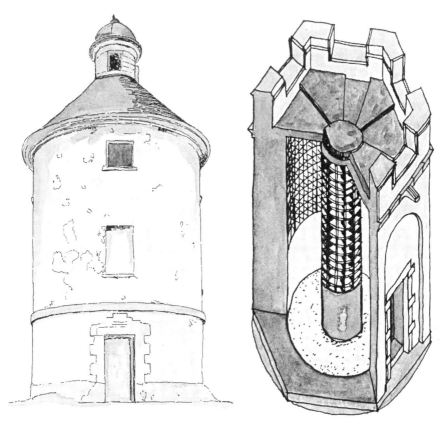

LEFT: *The Carloonan doocot at Inveraray Castle, Strathclyde, as it is today.*

RIGHT: *At Duff House, Grampian, the doocot is a hexagonal pavilion type with a flat roof of stone slabs supported by an internal column which is full of nesting boxes. The design may be by William Adam.*

Though highly influential, *The Country Seat* was just one of many manifestoes and pattern books published on the subject of the country house and its immediate surroundings.

Pleasure grounds, or 'policies', offered walks and rides in the vicinity of the country house and almost always included a walled garden and a stable block. During the eighteenth century one might also find a range of decorative little buildings ranging from a grotto lined with ammonites and tufa, to a hermitage with a resident hermit or a classical temple. Nineteenth-century structures tended to be more pragmatic and the rustic cottage for estate staff, the ornamental dairy and the icehouse buried in the ground were favoured.

Doocots were useful little buildings with decorative potential and their design and location relative to the mansion house came under increasing scrutiny. The most important decade in the development of the doocot as a self-consciously architectural structure was 1740-50. William Adam and Roger Morris were working at Whim House laying out elaborate pleasure grounds which included a doocot. Shortly afterwards, they collaborated with the Duke of Argyll to design the cylindrical Carloonan doocot at Inveraray Castle.

In 1743 Sir John Clerk of Penicuik was horrified to hear of the deliberate destruction (in order to repair a mill dam which was subsequently washed away) of the Temple of Terminus, an original Roman structure that had stood near Stirling, and he decided to have an exact replica built near Penicuik House. The resulting great dome, known colloquially as 'Arthur's O'on' (Arthur's Oven), was completed by 1760 and placed on top of his stable block, opposite a Gibbsean spire which had reputedly been designed for the local kirk and rejected by the elders as inappropriate. Inside Arthur's O'on was a purpose-built pigeonhouse with some 800 stone nesting boxes and a potence, still extant, with large wooden twenty-rung ladders. It was a great success and still houses a few birds. It was one of the first of many examples of the opportunities for architectural expression and formal or geometric experimentation that the provision of accommodation for pigeons could justify. Between 1748 and 1751 Sir John Clerk built a three-storey Flag Tower in his policies and included over 1300 nesting boxes in the unusual interior. The reason for this second doocot is described by Sir John: 'Last year 1750 and this I carried on the Tower on the top of the Knight's Law, and as I propose an ornament to the Country by it, I likewise have it in my view to make it beneficial to my family as a Dovecoat, that which I have by the House of Pennicuik being hurt by too many Trees

Penicuik House, Lothian. (Left) The 'Flag Tower' on Knight's Law looks like a Waterloo tower but it was designed by Sir John Clerk as a doocot with some 1400 nesting boxes on the first floor of the unusual interior. (Right) The court of offices was planned as a quadrangle including stables. Sir John Clerk added the spire above the main entry and the great dome of 'Arthur's O'on', a doocot, on one side.

LEFT: *The doocot at Westburn House, Strathclyde, is an octagonal pavilion standing on a hillock on Cambuslang golf course. When it was restored the rubble panels were rendered or 'harled'.*

RIGHT: *The only five-sided doocot in Scotland is at Nisbet Hill, Borders. The battlements, stone slab roof and large ball finial make this a unique structure.*

where Hawks and Gleds destroy the pigeons when they come out.'

From this time until the end of the century doocots were designed as innovative and decorative pavilions which could be seen and enjoyed relative to a designed landscape. Often the flexibility such design offered allowed architects to try out ideas which could subsequently be worked up at a larger scale in major new building projects. Between 1750 and 1800 pavilions of square, circular, octagonal, hexagonal and even pentagonal plan were decorated with pilasters, niches and conical or pyramidal roofs with lanterns or cupolas and weathervanes. Towards the end of the century the Gothick taste led to experiments with ogee roofs, quatrefoil windows, arrow slits and crenellations and occasionally the influence of a landowner who had recently returned to Scotland from India can perhaps be detected. There is even a proposal for a doocot in the Chinese pagoda style in a John Adam sketchbook.

Nevertheless, it would be wrong to think of all doocots principally as architectural statements. Many were no more than reasonably prestigious farm buildings in an age that cared about such things. Their charm lies in their individuality, frequently whimsical character and an attention to detail usually matched by a good standard of craftsmanship.

14

Around the middle of the eighteenth century an average doocot would have cost about £40.

The Carloonan doocot at Inveraray was completed in 1747 on axis with the old castle building at the point where the Garden Bridge was later built. By 1776 the architect Robert Mylne was commissioned to advise how it could be transformed into a temple, and he prepared a number of drawings showing proposals for a variety of arcades. Stone for the columns was quarried and work was about to begin on site when the Duke of Argyll fell ill and operations were stopped, never to be resumed. At roughly the same time the Adam brothers drew up designs for an octagonal-plan arcaded pigeonhouse for a man named Robert Boyle. The site was probably Shettleston, near Glasgow.

There are at least three possible reasons why Mylne may have been commissioned to change the appearance of the Carloonan doocot. Firstly, the existing structure, then a generation old, may simply have been considered not grand enough for such an important site, and the addition of an arcade would have made it far more impressive. Secondly, and more fancifully, Neil Munro's novel *The New Road* is based around a murder at the site of the Carloonan doocot, and if this were based on fact it would be as good an excuse as any to seek a change of appearance. Thirdly, Inveraray Castle was the centre of one of the most innovative and influential agricultural enterprises in Scotland, and the pioneering Duke of Argyll may have foreseen a time when pigeons were considered to do more harm than good, and pigeonhouses would be pulled down or converted into more useful structures.

LEFT: *Huntington House doocot, Lothian, is one of the finest examples from the mid eighteenth century. The vase shaped chimney is linked to a fireplace in the ground floor chamber. The pigeons lived on the first floor.*

RIGHT: *The doocot at Cadder House, Strathclyde, is now a feature on a golf course. The deep eaves and dressed stone pigeon ports and landing ledges may denote later additions to an existing structure.*

ABOVE: *Elvingston doocot, Lothian, is close to the house and decorated with battlements and an unusual cupola.*

ABOVE: *At Durie House is one of the big impressive doocots of Fife. There are some 1600 nesting boxes inside this great eight-sided tower.*

LEFT: *At Pittencrieff Park, Fife, the modern cupola contrasts with the gothick features of pointed arches, quatrefoil panels and 'Greek cross' arrowslit openings.*

16

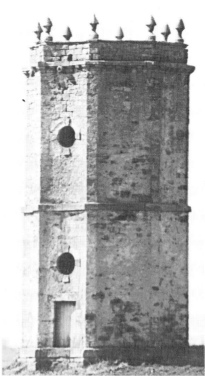

LEFT: *The doocot of Ormiston House, Lothian, is simple and elegant with squared dressed stonework or ashlar. This estate became well known through the agricultural improvements and innovations of John Cockburn in the early eighteenth century.*
RIGHT: *A large doocot in fields near Anstruther, Fife, with a good display of finials on the parapet.*

DISENCHANTMENT WITH PIGEONS

In the late sixteenth century John Napier, the inventor of logarithms, is said to have been so annoyed by the continual devastation of his crops by flocks of pigeons that he put down grain soaked in alcohol and bagged the drunken birds. In 1762 a landowner might have 'no dispute of qualifications' of a neighbour's right to build a pigeonhouse, but he might insist that it was not built near the centre of his fields. In the early 1790s Paine published his *Rights of Man*, drawing attention to social injustice, and many people must have viewed the large pigeonhouse as such an example of injustice. The 1793 Statistical Account for Inverness-shire notes that 'the laws respecting multures and pigeon houses are not founded in

equity. They are palpably oppressive.'

In 1796 it was estimated that in Midlothian pigeons had eaten enough grain for 3000 people and that in Fife some 300 private pigeonhouses offered accommodation to a breeding population of about 36,000 pairs of birds. Following protests by Scottish farmers, the Reverend Adam Philip lobbied for a pigeon tax. Two years earlier, in England, Humphry Repton wrote to a client advising him that his pigeonhouse was 'hardly worth consideration' and full of fleas. It was suggested that the pigeonhouse should be moved away from the dwelling house.

Concern about the quantities of food eaten by pigeons was heightened by the

17

restrictions imposed by the Napoleonic Wars from 1790 to 1810. Fortunately, the agricultural improvements that had been pursued so avidly in Scotland for fifty years were beginning to pay dividends, and as a result of advances in animal husbandry and the introduction of crops such as turnips it was now possible to keep livestock in quantity right through the winter. There was no longer any dependence on pigeons and there was a considerable amount of ill feeling towards them, at least from those who worked the land.

There are no records of wholesale pigeon killing or the large-scale demolition of doocots. It would be simple to disable a doocot by frightening away the birds and plugging the flight holes, and no doubt a lot of pigeons were shot and eaten.

Some doocots, however, were converted into pleasure houses or summerhouses offering shelter to visitors who wished to make a tour of the estate. A typical first step in such a conversion might be to plant a sapling of one of the new specimen trees from the New World alongside, such as the fashionable monkey puzzle. Dorothy Wordsworth visited Bonnington estate in 1803 and described a 'fog' house 'as snug as a bird's nest'. 'Fog' was a term for moss and the building was almost certainly a converted former doocot. By the time of her visit it resembled a scooped-out haystack furnished with table and chairs neatly finished in moss.

Robert Smirke is credited with the design in 1825 of the thatched *cottage ornee* at Mellerstain, but this almost certainly originated as a doocot too. Stow doocot was used as a dwelling by the navvies who built the Edinburgh to Galashiels road, and Loretto doocot was converted into a memorial tower for a deceased headmaster.

LEFT: *The eighteenth-century doocot at Colstoun House, Lothian, now forms a fine end to nineteenth-century farmworkers' dwellings.*

RIGHT: *A simple one-chambered farmyard doocot by the road at Bolton, Lothian.*

A farmyard doocot near Culross, Fife.

FARMYARDS AND COURTS OF OFFICE

Throughout the nineteenth century those pigeonhouses that were built were almost exclusively designed in association with farmyards or courts of offices which would contain a wide range of farm facilities. On occasions, for example at Colstoun House, an eighteenth-century pigeon house has been almost swallowed up by nineteenth-century development. The doocot might be placed at the centre of a quadrangle or circle of buildings, or located above an archway.

As early as 1725 *The Sportsman's Dictionary* suggested that one 'plant the pigeonhouse in the middle of a courtyard and near enough to the house that the master of the family may keep in awe those who go in or out', clear evidence of the importance attached to security.

The pigeonhouse could be placed at the centre of an existing farmyard to form a feature or designed as the centrepoint of a 'model farm' development. Towards the end of the eighteenth century a number of financial incentives were introduced to encourage landowners to improve their stables and 'offices' and one result was a series of proposals for architect-designed 'model farms'.

The Adam brothers prepared drawings in 1789 for an important project, described as a 'Court of Offices in the Castle Stile for John Johnstone Esq, proposed to be built in Alva. This building contains stables for all the Coach and riding Horses, with Coach Houses for 4 Carriages, Brewhouse, Bakehouse, Laundry and Wash House, Cow House, Dairy, Henhouse, Stewards House, Pig House, Slaughter House, Cart Shed, Smith and Carpenters Shops, with all the yards necessary to the different offices and Pryvys for the servants of each, with a Dung Pit in the centre of this Court covered over with a Pigeon House. And in those parts of the building that are raised 2 Stories, are got rooms for lodging the servants near the offices which they superintend and to which they belong.' This project was unfortunately never realised, possibly because of the Napoleonic Wars. Daniel Mathie was another architect who prepared schemes with a pigeonhouse as the central feature of a court of offices or as part of a building designed especially for fowls at a time when theorists disapproved of free-range hens.

Early nineteenth-century pragmatists increasingly saw the pigeonhouse as a

LEFT: *A farmyard doocot near St Boswells with a slated glover and a wide landing perch of dressed stone corbelled out from the sides.*

BELOW LEFT: *One of the best and most consistent examples of a doocot at the centre of a quadrangle of offices is at Kinross, Central. It is located much closer to the main house than to the home farm.*

BELOW RIGHT: *At Keith Marischal, Lothian, an octagonal eighteenth-century doocot stands at the centre of the court of offices.*

ABOVE: *The doocot built into a courtyard at The Hirsel, Borders.*

BELOW LEFT: *The doocot at Denbie House, Dumfries, is a little octagonal pavilion with a datestone of 1775 and a nicely detailed blind cupola. Within it are some 250 brick and slate nesting boxes.*

BELOW RIGHT: *The courtyard of the home farm at Saltoun Hall, Lothian, is dominated by this cupola on an octagonal base, which is a doocot.*

21

building to be combined with the pheasantry or poultry house, and a few impressive and extravagant schemes were mooted, most notably by the Earl of Aberdeen at Haddo House and by the Earl of Cassillis at Culzean. But by 1820 trelliswork, lattices and rustic timber were becoming the predominant materials for garden buildings. There was no longer any desire or need for pigeons, and designers began to explore the architectural potential of the mausoleum as a suitable pavilion for experimental sculpting and modelling, and this, with its more serious and heroic connotations, was well suited for the advent of the Greek Revival style in Scotland. The nineteenth-century pigeonhouse would never achieve the same entertainment value as could be had from the contem-

porary menagerie, the aviary, the volary or vivarium and the exhibition of strange beasts and swans. One of the few known extant large pigeonhouses from this time is Archibald Simpson's design of 1828 at Stracathro House.

Where the pigeonhouse was not the central feature of a courtyard, it was often placed in a cupola over the main entrance arch. This was a practice common through most of the nineteenth century and it allowed for a few, mainly decorative, pigeons with their comforting cooing noises and provided a distinctive dome or spire visible across the surrounding fields. The structures at Saltoun Hall and Rosebery Mains are good examples. Where a pigeonhouse was thought to be inappropriate, a belfry or clock-tower might be used as a substitute.

LEFT: *Rosebery Mains, Lothian. Dummy windows at first floor level of this amazing structure front a doocot.*

RIGHT: *Stenton church tower, Lothian, adjacent to the present church tower, was converted for pigeons and is still populated by them.*

ABOVE LEFT: *An early nineteenth-century doocot at Lesmurdie House, Grampian, of rather severe appearance.*

ABOVE RIGHT: *This steading at Edrom, Borders, boasts a lovely entrance arch with a datestone of 1874 above the pigeon ports.*

BELOW: *This doocot at Stracathro, Tayside, with low-pitched roof, bracketed wide eaves and air of restraint is by Archibald Simpson, a proponent of the 'Greek Revival' style.*

Near Lundin Tower, Fife, is a medieval chapel which was converted into a doocot about 1800.

COMPOSITE AND MISCELLANEOUS STRUCTURES

Freestanding beehive and lectern pigeon-houses, with their straightforward chambers, were rarely used for anything other than accommodating pigeons. But pavilion structures, which frequently had more than one storey, presented opportunities for other uses.

Henhouse, wine cellar, potting shed, donkey house and granary are all typical examples of uses for the lower level of a two-storey pavilion-type pigeonhouse, and several examples include fireplaces. At Murdostoun there is an egg-shaped icehouse in the lower storey and the whole structure is crowned with an ogee roof. On the isle of Stroma the pigeon-house is combined with a ground-level burial vault, and Dishan Tower at Balfour Castle on the isle of Shapinsay was reputedly converted to include a salt-water shower ('douche house') and a doocot. Invermay has the combination of pigeonhouse and rustic dairy.

These structures were all largely purpose-built. Some of the more bizarre structures are the result of adapting

existing buildings to house pigeons, and examples range from the use of converted church towers such as Stenton and Monifieth to the adaptation of redundant battlemented windpumps and the conversion of windmills. At Lundin Tower a medieval chapel was 'restored' in the Gothick style in about 1800 and turned into a pigeonhouse. At Dunipace, Edmonstone and Sherrif Old Hall the stair towers of otherwise demolished ancient houses were fitted with nesting boxes, and at the last site sixteenth-century gunloops can still be seen in the walls.

At Amisfield there was a pigeonhouse in one of the four great stone drums which form the corner pavilions to Scotland's most impressive neo-classical walled garden. At Lochend Castle a sixteenth-century doocot is said to have been altered and used as a kiln during the plague of 1645.

Sometimes alterations to a pigeonhouse consisted of no more than adding a little further accommodation. Reused

This doocot at Sherrif Old Hall, Lothian, was once the main stair tower of a sixteenth-century castle, demolished in the 1830s. Gunloops and old openings can be seen in the walls. The inside is circular and lined with some 850 wooden nesting boxes; the potence is extant, the glover is recent. The doocot is constructed of red sandstone and basalt.

masonry has sometimes been built into pigeonhouses where additional decoration was required, and since this includes dated panels one should not assume that a date displayed on such a building is the year of its construction. Nesting boxes made of timber by the estate carpenter, rather than masonry slabs built into pigeonhouse walls, are sometimes an indication that a building has been converted to a pigeonhouse but are not conclusive evidence.

The great neo-classical walled garden at Amisfield, Lothian, was built in 1783. One of the four stone drums which formed corner pavilions was used as a doocot, with 1180 wooden nesting boxes. Pigeon entry was from above. (The roof structure is no longer extant.)

25

Simple gate piers once marked this entry to the estate at Balcaskie, Fife. In 1911 the architect Sir Robert Lorimer added the twin doocots and screen walls to make an entry of much more character. Pigeons from these structures were still being eaten in the 1940s.

THE TWENTIETH CENTURY

The Edwardians were very conscious of the decorative potential of doves in their sophisticated granite stable blocks or in a setting beside a croquet lawn. At Manderston a decorative masonry pavilion with leaded lights and a pyramidal roof offers a few nesting boxes for fantails, and at Melsetter on Hoy W. R. Lethaby included a tea-house and doocot in the garden wall. It was more common to restrict facilities to a small timber construction which could be hung on an outside wall.

Just before the First World War, several noteworthy Scottish architects produced designs for doocots. Drawings by Joass show the simple 'barrel on a pole' solution and Charles Rennie Mackintosh sketched a little thatched shelter for doves. Sir Robert Lorimer capitalised on the existing gateway at Balcaskie House and turned it into a tour de force: twin pavilions provide a unique and memorable entry to this fine estate. At Crathes

Castle the seventeenth-century doocot was moved into the walled garden to provide a focal point as part of major alterations in 1937.

The twentieth century has not, however, been an easy time for the Scottish country house, still less for the little buildings which once were so important in the running of estates. Wars, taxes, development of land and fundamental changes in society have had profound effects, and scores of country houses have been demolished. Instead of finding the laird's pigeonhouse near his fields, one frequently has to look elsewhere; thus Daldowie doocot is at a sewage works, Westquarter doocot is hemmed in by houses, and other favoured sites are golf courses and country parks. Of the houses they once served there is often no sign.

With increasing interest in historic gardens and a general movement towards conservation since the 1960s, much has already been done towards keeping Scot-

ABOVE: *The National Trust for Scotland own Boath Doocot, Highland, which stands on the mound from which Montrose directed the battle of Auldearn.*

BELOW: *A 'fuie' was originally a small timber construction with a few nesting boxes that could be hung on an outside wall. This fancy example at Kellie Castle, Fife, is probably by Sir Robert Lorimer, about 1910. The feature on the left is a sundial.*

tish doocots in good repair, though there is always the danger of over-enthusiastic conservation leaving an old building looking so well scrubbed that all the romantic patina of age has disappeared.

Doocots at Boath and Phantassie are owned by the National Trust for Scotland, others such as Tealing and West-quarter are classified as Ancient Monuments, and those such as Muiravonside and Cumbernauld have been restored with the help of local authority grant aid. A number of estates in private ownership have made efforts to keep doocots on their land in good repair, and it is possible to visit many of these as part of Scotland's Gardens Scheme.

Despite these hopeful signs there is a danger that a few well preserved doocots will be all that is left; the great majority, well loved landmarks, will have crumbled beyond repair.

RIGHT: *The structure at Bowerbutts, Fife, is a combined doocot and icehouse dating from the eighteenth century.*

LEFT: *The doocot at Crathes Castle, Grampian, may well be of seventeenth-century origin but it was moved and renovated in the 1930s to provide a focal point at one corner of a flower garden.*

A typical derelict lectern doocot.

FURTHER READING

Beaton, E. *The Doocots of Moray.* Moray Field Club, 1978.
Clerk, J. *Clerk of Penicuik's Memoires 1676-1755.* Publications of the Scottish History Society (volume 13), 1892.
Cooke, A. O. *A Book of Dovecotes.* T. N. Foulis, 1920.
Fenton, A., and Walker, B. *The Rural Architecture of Scotland.* John Donald, 1981.
Lindsay, I., and Cosh, M. *Inveraray and the Dukes of Argyll.* Edinburgh University Press, 1973.
Peterkin, G. A. G. *Scottish Dovecotes.* W. Culross and Son, 1980.
Ritchie, A. *Exploring Scotland's Heritage: Orkney and Shetland.* HMSO/RCAHM(S), 1985.
Robertson, A. N. Article in Volume 25 of *The Book of the Old Edinburgh Club.* T. and A. Constable, 1945.
Robinson, J. M. *Georgian Model Farms 1700-1846.* Oxford University Press, 1984.
In addition, there are many references to Scottish doocots in the relevant Pevsner volumes, and also in the volumes of the Royal Commission on the Ancient and Historical Monuments of Scotland, which are published by Her Majesty's Stationery Office.

GAZETTEER OF DOOCOTS

All the doocots listed here are believed to be extant at the time of publication, though a number are derelict. Please note that at the time of writing only those examples marked with an asterisk are on land sometimes open to the public; most of the others are on private land and permission from the owner should be sought before seeking access. This list is not intended to be exhaustive but it serves to indicate the extensive variety of doocots in Scotland. Grid references are given in brackets.

BEEHIVE AND MODIFIED BEEHIVE TYPE
Aberdour, Fife (NT 192855), sixteenth century, associated with castle.
Auchmacoy, Grampian (NK 993309), 1638 onwards, gabled chamber over tun belly.
Crossraguel Abbey*, Strathclyde (NS 281078), sixteenth century, first floor chamber.
Dirleton*, Lothian (NT 520839). Built into castle walls.
Dolphinton, Lothian (NT 385730). Three stage rubble type.
Dunure*, Strathclyde (NS 253158). Four stage structure by coast.
Freswick, Highland (ND 365678).
Gordonstoun, Grampian (NJ 184690), late sixteenth century.
Hall of Rendall, Orkney (HY 422207), sixteenth and seventeenth centuries.
Luffness, Lothian (NT 485819). 500 nesting boxes, billet cornice.
Mertoun House, Borders (NT 615320), dated 1576.
Newark Castle, Strathclyde (NS 328745).
Nunraw Abbey, Lothian (NT 595720), sixteenth century onwards.
Phantassie*, Lothian (NT 600785), sixteenth century, unusual hood.
Prestonpans*, Lothian (NT 385738), probably sixteenth century, recently restored.
West Meikle Pinkerton, Lothian (NT 720756), sixteenth century.

LECTERN AND SQUARE-PLAN RIDGE-ROOF TYPE
Addistoun, Lothian (NT 157698). Two chambers, one access door.
Ballindalloch, Grampian (NJ 178367), dated 1696. Ridge roof with timber glover.
Bowerhouse, Lothian (NT 672767).
Burgie, Grampian (NJ 093593), late sixteenth century.
Charleton, Fife (NO 460038). Single chamber with 'dormer' pigeon ports.
Drummond Castle*, Tayside (NN 850915), built adjacent to house.
Drumquhassle, Central (NS 483871), dated 1711. Square plan, brick nestboxes.
Dumfries House, Strathclyde (NS 543205). Fine armorial panel over entry.
Earlshall*, Fife (NO 465210), about 1599, a feature at end of avenue.
Finavon*, Tayside (NO 490578), seventeenth century, restored 1979. (Museum.)
Glamis Castle*, Tayside (NO 385480), seventeenth century, two chambered.
Johnstounburn, Lothian (NT 462620), eighteenth century, ornamental structure.
Kailzie, Borders (NT 265392), dated 1698, one chambered.
Laraben, Central (NS 626954), later eighteenth century, unusual brick structure.
Leitcheston, Grampian (NJ 399626), seventeenth century, four chambered.
Malleny*, Lothian (NT 162657).
Muiravonside*, Lothian (NS 965753), seventeenth century type, possibly much later, restored 1982.
Naughton House, Fife (NO 374246), about 1750, two chambered.
Newliston, Lothian (NT 110735), early eighteenth century, converted about 1980.
New Spynie, Grampian (NJ 183643), about 1600. Ridge-roofed structure.
Pencaitland*, Lothian (NT 450910).
Pinkie House*, Lothian (NT 356728), dated 1607. Panels and marriage stones.
Saltcoats Castle*, Lothian (NT 485823), late sixteenth century.
Spott House, Lothian (NT 674760). Large two-chambered structure.
Tantallon Castle*, Lothian (NT 595845), seventeenth century, two chambered.
Tealing Home Farm*, Tayside (NO 418383), 1595. Ridge-roofed structure.
Westquarter*, Central (NS 913787), eighteenth century. Fine armorial panel.

PAVILION TYPE

*Boath**, Highland (NH 916556), circular, in NTS ownership.
Bolton, Lothian (NT 511712), circular, late eighteenth century.
Busta, Shetland (HU 347669), circular, early eighteenth century.
Cadder House, Strathclyde (NS 620731), circular, late eighteenth century.
Camis Eskan, Strathclyde (NS 345778), octagonal, late eighteenth century.
Carron House, Central (NS 897826), octagonal, about 1800, decorative parapet.
Castle Huntly, Tayside (NO 302292), square, seventeenth century, turrets.
Colstoun House, Lothian (NT 523731), circular, eighteenth century.
*Corstorphine**, Lothian (NT 173728), circular, sixteenth century.
*Crathes Castle**, Grampian (NO 733968), square, seventeenth century, rebuilt 1937.
Crossburn, Strathclyde (NS 540746), square.
*Cumbernauld**, Strathclyde (NS 778762), circular, sixteenth century, converted 1731, restored 1975.
Daldowie, Strathclyde (NS 675632), circular, domed roof.
Denbie House, Dumfries (NY 110731), octaganol, dated 1775.
Dougalston House, Strathclyde (NS 569752), octagonal.
*Duff House**, Grampian (NJ 691634), octagonal, early eighteenth century.
*Dunrobin**, Highland (ND 850020), square, with pyramidal roof.
Durie, Fife (NO 373026), octagonal, late eighteenth century, over 1600 nestboxes.
Edzell, Tayside (NO 582692), square, ridge roof and turrets.
Elvingston House, Lothian (NT 470750), circular, about 1850. Cupola and battlements.
Huntington House, Lothian (NT 475750), square, about 1750.
*Inveraray**, Strathclyde (NN 087090), circular, 1747.
Kininvie, Grampian (NJ 3194410), circular, eighteenth century.
Lesmurdie House, Grampian (NJ 225636), octagonal, early nineteenth century.
Longformacus, Borders (NT 672571), circular, eighteenth century.
Monteviot, Borders (NT 648259), circular, nineteenth century.
Nisbet Hill, Borders (NT 799512), pentagonal, eighteenth century.
Ormiston, Lothian (NT 425675), circular, dressed ashlar flat roof.
Orton, Grampian (NJ 314534), circular, early eighteenth century.
*Pittencrieff Park**, Fife (NT 085872), circular, with gothick dressings.
Saltoun Hall, Lothian (NT 455682), square, with gothick decoration.
Strathleven House, Strathclyde (NS 392783), circular, eighteenth century.
Westburn House, Strathclyde (NS 641598), octagonal, eighteenth century, restored about 1975.

MISCELLANEOUS DOOCOTS

Aden, Grampian (NJ 981478), top of tower dominating court of offices, about 1800.
Amisfield, Lothian (NT 531745), the south-eastern of four great stone drums which form corner pavilions to the large neo-classical walled garden built in 1783.
Balcaskie, Fife (NO 524037), seventeenth-century gate piers with later addition of twin pavilioned doocots designed by Sir Robert Lorimer about 1911.
Balfour, Highland (HY 479170), combined doocot and salt-water shower, restored in the nineteenth century.
Bowbutts, Fife (NT 316942), eighteenth-century combined doocot and icehouse.
Carskie, Strathclyde (NR 655079), pair of twin octagonal doocots, one late eighteenth century, the other a nineteenth-century copy.
Darleith, Strathclyde (NS 345810), construction with conical roofed circular tower at end of former avenue.
Edrom, Borders (NT 435562), doocot over entry to court of offices.
Hawthornden, Lothian (NT 281639), doocot formed in natural cavern.
*The Hirsel**, Borders (NT 831422), doocot within court of offices.
Invermay, Tayside (NO 065168), combined doocot and rustic dairy built about 1802.
Keith Marischal, Lothian (NT 469665), octagonal doocot within eighteenth-century court of offices.

Kinross, Central (NO 125023), circular doocot within eighteenth-century court of offices. Probably the best extant example of this type.

Luffness, Lothian (NT 490708), doocot formed in Italianate water tower.

Lundin, Fife (NO 395037), medieval chapel converted to doocot about 1800.

*Manderston**, Borders (NT 821547), small Edwardian pavilion by croquet lawn.

Megginch, Tayside (NO 242245), Gothick centrepiece of early nineteenth-century court of offices.

Mellerstain, Borders (NT 653396), *cottage ornée* probably converted by Robert Smirke about 1825 from earlier doocot.

Melsetter, Hoy, Orkney (ND 270893), design by Lethaby in garden wall, 1898.

Murdostoun, Strathclyde (NS 832578), combined doocot and icehouse built about 1790.

Papple, Lothian (NT 591732), doocot over main entry arch to steading.

Penicuik, Lothian (NT 220597), 'Flag Tower' built about 1750 by Sir John Clerk on top of hill.

Penicuik, Lothian (NT 216594), copy of Roman shrine built above stable block about 1760 by Sir John Clerk, nicknamed 'Arthur's O'on' (Oven).

Rosebery, Lothian (NT 305575), doocot in spire dominating steading built about 1800.

Saltoun Hall, Lothian (NT 452681), doocot in dome above steading built about 1790.

Sherrif Old Hall, Lothian (NT 316681), doocot in former stair tower of sixteenth-century house. Square exterior, circular interior, wooden boxes.

*Stenton Church**, Lothian (NT 632746), doocot in church tower.

Stracathro, Tayside (NO 627653), 'Greek Revival' style doocot built about 1828 by Archibald Simpson.

Stroma, Highland (ND 450779), combined doocot and burial vault dated 1677.

Symbister House, Shetland (HU 542621), doocot towers in stables, about 1830.

Urquhart Manse, Grampian (NJ 283627), small doocot built of cob.

Wemyss Castle, Fife (NT 329956), eighteenth-century battlemented tower, former windpump, converted during nineteenth century to doocot.

At Manderston, Borders, the doocot is a small chamber in the roof of a tiny pavilion by the croquet lawn.